THE GROWTH PAIN GAVE ME

What pain planted, time allowed to grow

A Poetry Collection

By Omarion Phillips

First Edition

ISBN: ____________ (paperback)

Published by
GrowthFrame Studio LLC

Visit the author online:
www.GrowthFrameStudio.com

Printed in the United States of America

GrowthFrame Studio

GrowthFrame Studio exists to build growth, not merely speak about it.

Growth represents transformation — the lessons, the becoming.

Frame represents the structure that holds it together: the strength of construction, the focus of a picture frame, and the motion of a film frame.

Studio is the creative space where these elements are shaped into art people can feel and see themselves in.

Cinematic Growth. Written in Pressure.

DEDICATION

To my mother,

whose love carried me through storms I never
spoke about, whose strength became the soil I rooted
rooted myself in.

To my father,

who wasn't always beside me,
yet still taught me lessons from a distance—
lessons about resilience, about becoming,
about shaping myself into more than what I came from.

To my brothers,

who grew alongside me through quiet battles and
loud moments, who shared the weight of becoming men
in a world that demanded more from us than we ever
said out loud.

To my friends,

whose family I chose, who stood with
me through distance, darkness, and
growth—thank you for giving me
reason to keep blooming.

TABLE OF CONTENTS

*What pain planted,
time allowed to grow.*

SECTION I
SOIL

Origins, Absorption, Damage before choice

The Soil of Unspoken Things

There was a time when I was nothing—
nothing more than a blank page
in a blank book,
still smooth,
still unmarked,
still uncreased.

Before I learned the power
of naming myself,
I was only a silence
waiting to be written
into existence.

In a world like ours,
blank pages never stay pure for long.
Conservative about the marks I left,
yet even my own hand slipped
off the page—
scribbling lines I didn't understand,
inking truths
I wasn't ready to hold.

Trying to repair
the stained pages of my life,
fingerprints began to smudge.
Suddenly my smooth edges
creased beneath the weight
of names, expectations,
and chapters written
before I learned
to write myself.

Devoured by lessons
I was too young to understand,
their weight settling in my bones
long before I knew their names.

Every truth I didn't want to hold
left its mark,
every mistake I didn't choose
pressed itself into my pages—
building a book of burdens
I never asked to write.

Still, the weight of this book
shaped the story—
highlighting what rose
and what collapsed,
settling into the darkness
the way roots do
when they first learn the ground.

And like roots deep in the dirt,
I stayed grounded—
surrounded by things
that navigated the soil
with an ease I never had.

My pages filled with the earth
that shaped me,
growing inward into silence,
into pressure,
into the empty spaces
I never knew how to fill.

Brewing in the ground
I once found too deep to name,
I trembled beneath a quiet storm—
rain soaking into my roots,
soft at first,
but even the gentlest rain
can strike hard
when the soil is already heavy.

And still, the soil settled deeper,
packing its lessons tight around me—
not to trap me,
but to shape the emptiness inside
into something that could hold weight one day.

Every grain of soil
became a quiet reminder
that becoming begins
long before anyone sees it.

I wasn't meant to rise yet—
the soil was still teaching me
what roots must know:
that darkness is the first home,
and pressure is the first teacher,
and every beginning
starts beneath the weight
that tries to break it.

Soaked in Soil

Before the world ever touched me,
I grew in the dark—
touched not by my own thoughts,
but by someone else's breath and blood,
feeding me through a cord
that built my core,
undeveloped,
yet developing.

The darkness held me,
not as an enemy
but as a quiet guardian—
a silence thick enough
to steady my breathing.
Warmth wrapped around me
with a purity I didn't understand,
a kindness older than language,
a heart beating for me
long before I knew
how to survive on my own.

My beginning was much like a seed
separating from its maker—
fragile and blind
to what was waiting for me.

Dropping into a world
directed by forces uncontrollable
and unknown to me—
not by the choices I made,
but by the choices of others.
That's just how gravity works.

Buried deep within the soil,
the world didn't just press—
it collapsed onto me,
layer after layer
of weight I hadn't earned yet.
The earth was cold,
clinging to my skin
with a loneliness that felt alive,
its damp grip tightening
as if it meant to keep me hidden.
Is this what growth requires—
to be crushed
before reaching upward?

A fracture formed in me—
not to break me,
but to free me,
to make room
for what was coming.
My roots pushed
against the weight above,
and still,
I wasn't done growing.

Roots Watered in Pain

In the beginning,
I grew on water meant to drown me.
They fed me anyway—
urging me to absorb
everything poured over my small roots,
washing me in hurt and quiet suffering
until it sank into the soil,
deep into the person I was becoming
long before I knew I'd been poisoned.

Pain became my source of water—
my strength,
the first thing I learned to drink,
and the only thing poured into me
without hesitation.

In time,
I became the hurt—
the poison that soaked my soil.
My roots grounded themselves
in the same pain that killed me slowly,
bending and curling around
every jagged stone life buried beside me.
My wounds shaped me,
but I chose the shape—
teaching my fragile, trembling roots
to stand firm in soil
that was never meant
to keep me alive.

Months, days, even years
it took me to understand
that not every plant grows in the soil it's given.
Was this normal?
Was this how it was meant to be—
the water I drank offered for growth,
or meant to shatter me
and return me to the soil
that tried to extinguish
the life I sought to live?

A burial covered in dirt
and poisoned by water—
I never saw who poured the first cup,
only that it came again and again,
soaking me deeper in the pain
that tried to uproot me.

And for years,
my silence and that poisoned water
quietly shaped the rhythm of my breath,
and taught me how long a heart can mistake survival
for being loved.

My roots, watered in pain,
poisoned in the ground that raised me,
still survived—
a beat that grew stronger
than the roots themselves.
They reached for what lived beyond the earth,
and I learned to pull strength
from the place meant to devour me—
to swallow me in its soil
and drown me in its darkness.

Still, I rose from the ruined earth,
soaked in truths clearer than they had ever been,
carrying the proof that even a seed left for dead can choose its own becoming.

Before the Sun Slips Away

Long in wait, I waited to play—
for who could catch me
on this blessed day?

Down and around,
I jumped and played,
until the sun
slowly slipped away.

Then came night,
arriving too fast.
I jumped once more,
then slid, breathless.
I said my goodbyes—
for who could know
the next time
I'd be back outside?

Weak and tired,
I carried myself,
until I reached
one blessed home—
warmth leaking
beneath its door.
Oh, how I longed
for just a little more.

Weakened, I stepped
on the cold, cold floor,
just to reach the kitchen
for something warm.

Home at last,
I cheered with delight.
Bedtime was calling
from left and right.

Laying upon
my silken dress,
my eyes grew warm
with needed rest.
For now, I play
within my dreams,
until the sun
rises with me.

When it does,
I wait again—
only to find
my friends in wait.

What Grew From the Broken Ground

What grew from the broken ground—
a ground full of poisoned memories
and hard truths—
still found a way to rise.
A figure the soil never predicted to hold,
pushing through the cracks
that opened beneath me,
lifting me into a world
I didn't yet trust to carry me.

Something rose from the rubble
of what had failed me,
a quiet echo
that even damage
can grow a direction of its own.

I was formed by every moment
I fought to survive,
shaped by the weight
the world pressed onto me.
Every crack the earth left behind
etched itself into who I was becoming,
and the pieces the soil stripped from me
found their way into my roots—
ghosts from a poisoned ground
still clinging to the man I rose to be.

But rising came with a cost—
every inch upward
carrying a weight I'd long outgrown,
a weight that reminded me
this was not the end.
The poison I'd risen from

pressed itself into my chest,
lingering like a bruise
the world could not see—
a quiet testament
that even progress
can carry its own ache.

Still, something in me kept rising—
not clean, not whole,
but certain in its direction,
certain that the poison inside me
had become my own,
molding me into a man
led by the mistakes
buried long before him.

And though the ground behind me
remains broken,
the cracks embedded in it live on—
reminders that even from damaged earth,
a man can learn
to stand.

SECTION II
SHADOWS

Exposure, endurance, survival in silence

Where the dark lives

Down in the deep—
whether it lived in my mind
or in my soul—
I felt what they called
depression.

A stage in life so deep,
deep enough
to take control.

Forever growing,
never showing,
always lurking
with no one knowing.

Countless tries
to bring light to the dark,
yet only some
are saved from this part.

Those who received
what little was given
felt something within
strong enough
to alter the written.

Pondering in the dark,
lying still,
my mind sharp—
and nearly killed.

Deep it goes,
from head to toe,
a downcast weight
that takes control.

Joyful smiles,
hollow and stolen—
only a few
know the truth beneath them.

Twisted knots
hanging from the ceiling...
this path
leads to one last feeling.

Deep,
where the dark lives
inside.

Beneath the Bones

Being trapped in your own mind
will be the thing that ultimately breaks you.

There is a place beneath the bones,
where sunlight forgets to reach—
a place so far, so dark, so deep
I often forget how to sleep.

Tossing and turning
in a place where ambition comes to die
and shadows still thrive.
Where silence hums like a wound,
and every heartbeat sinks
into its dying tomb.
This place, this darkness—
it's called the Sunken Place.

Hope—
neither stranger nor friend—
decays as the silence
begins to thin.
Crying, screaming—
it all starts to fade,
while you foolishly hope
it'll come back someday.

Bones crack and snap,
just like the feeling
you once held back.
Buried in the soil
that now holds you down,
feeding the roots of everything you lost—
a tic for tac.

Yet a feeling remains—
not hope, not life,
but the memory of wanting to be.
It sits in this place,
small and hollow,
digging within the grave
I built for myself—
dark, cold,
and sometimes hopeless.

This place
is called
the Sunken Place.

The Silence That Shaped Me

Silence—
something I didn't know I needed.

Always present,
never empty.
It had weight.

It lingered in rooms
long after people left,
closing itself around
whatever it could,
letting me breathe inside its power
as it pressed against my chest
like a breath held too long.

It watched me
and spoke even less,
hinting at something
I never learned to name.

What it taught me
was this—
quiet can feel crowded
and still be ignored.

I didn't choose silence—
it chose me,
and I learned how to live inside it.

I learned unanswered questions
were never meant to be answered.
So I stopped explaining myself,
let quiet carry
what words would only cheapen.

My silence grew—
disciplined,
contained,
dangerous.
I learned when speaking
cost more
than it gave back.

So I swallowed reactions,
bit down on my words,
measured every breath.
I made room for the quiet to spread,
let moments pass untouched,
learning that survival
often sounded
like nothing at all.

After a while,
silence was no longer a choice
but a habit.

It became my power
when everything else felt weak—
thorns on a rose,
sharp enough
to keep distance.

No one questioned
the quiet I wielded.
They spoke around me,
over me,
as if my silence meant agreement,
as if my stillness meant absence.

I watched conversations move on
without noticing
I had something to say—
and I let them.

My words never disappeared—
my silence grew.

It settled into my body,
took residence in my chest,
filled the spaces
where truth wanted to live.

Every conversation,
spoken or swallowed,
pressed inward,
stacking weight on weight
until even breathing
felt like a negotiation.

It shaped me—
won't say silence saved me.
I won't say it ruined me.
It taught me
to choose what I speak into,
to understand
that words carry weight

It shaped me—
taught me control,
restraint,
how to endure
without being seen.

I never learned how to break the silence—
only how to become someone
it could grow in,
and live inside.

What I Learned in the Quiet

The quiet—
a hard slap to the face,
never gentle.

It didn't comfort me—
it instructed.

Teaching lessons
I thought I already knew,
revealing what remained
when voices disappeared,
when the guidance of others
no longer lingered.

When quiet crept under doors,
through dark rooms,
not asking permission—
just because it could.

My own thoughts
closing in.

In the quiet,
there was no one
to correct me—
only consequences
waiting to be understood.

Silence gave me space
to see my own faults,
to face my wrongs
without distraction.

It was no game—
it was a lesson,
soaked in the value
of the quiet itself.

In many ways,
it was the teacher
that slapped your hand
when you reached wrong.
The quiet handed me
the pieces of myself
I kept excusing.

No one else to blame.
No noise loud enough
to drown my own thoughts,
my own decisions—
they lingered,
even when unwanted.

The quiet taught me
how I mistook endurance
for strength,
and distance
for control.

It didn't hide my mistakes.
It let me see myself clearly
and left me there
to sit with it—
in the quiet place.

Knowing didn't bring relief—
it brought weight
I wasn't ready to lift.

Truth, once covered by darkness,
was revealed by silence.
There was no unseeing it,
no returning
to the person I was
before I understood
my part in it.

Every mistake carried a name now—
names I grew too familiar with,
names that echoed in the dark
when everything else fell quiet.

The quiet stayed.
It showed me its value,
reminding me that
some lessons,
once learned,
do not loosen their grip.

I didn't come out of the quiet better—
just clearer.

Clear about what I carried,
what I avoided,
what I allowed to stay
longer than it should have.

The quiet didn't forgive me.
It didn't condemn me either.

It simply remained,
making sure I remembered
who I became
when no one else was watching.

I still move with it beside me,
not as comfort,
but as proof
that growth doesn't always arrive gently—
sometimes it leaves you heavier,
and awake.

Deep Breaths

Sometimes I have to stop and breathe—
not because I'm calm,
but because I'm trying to be.

Deep breaths — 1, 2, 3.

I count the weight inside me:
pain and anger washing over,
flooding every thought within.

One breath—maybe more—
keeping the things I shouldn't say
swallowed in the storm.

Slow breaths that deepen slightly,
stirring the whirling sea inside me.
Even the ocean can't stay silent forever;
the quiet never stays quiet for long—
not when her voice still echoes
in places it doesn't belong.

Deep breaths again — 1, 2, 3.

I close my eyes and she's everywhere—
in the calm,
in the chaos,
in the space between each breath.

The waves still crash but never reach shore,
a storm in motion—unspent, endless.
Every breath a fight against the tide,
every thought a pull I can't escape.

Finally, a steady breath — 1, 2, 3.

The storm still swirls,
ferocious around me.
Waves rise and fall—
yet I stand, anchored in myself,breathing through the storm.

Alive.

Ink Aged in Pain

Aged in pain—
I aged, and so did the ache,
stretching across my heart
like an old bandage of time,
killing me slow—
but never slower
than the pain that came with it.
Each day it etched its name
into my chest,
a routine carved deeper
than my breath itself.

My mind forever carried
the thoughts of my pain
and the weight of memories
that settled deep in my head—
nights aging into walls,
dry, rotten, tired of the abuse,
yet still forced to stand.
And there I stood with them,
silent, unmoving,
aged in pain beside the ruin.

Time—my greatest enemy,
second only to myself,
turns the pages of my life slowly,
exposing memories
on dry-rotting paper.
Ink spills across each thin sheet,
savoring the moments
aged in my pain.
The pages speak of things
I tried to bury,
yet Time reads them aloud

in my darkest hours—
reminding me that pain
either grows with me,
or rots beneath the soil
as something I must outgrow.

Pages once fresh and new,
now aged by time,
loosened from their spine.
Ink, dark and blackened,
bled across each page,
staining the history
it tried to preserve.

A book once light
now grew heavy—
not from the words written,
but from the ones
that could never be erased—
a story damaged,
its pages torn.

In the end,
every book finds its final chapter—
pages that shaped the story,
pages that hid its pain,
its struggles,
its memories within.

Each page pressed with ink,
a fingerprint of a life
I once couldn't escape,
but slowly outgrew with time.

It grew with me—
not as a friend,
nor as an enemy,
but as a lesson;
a subtitle in the chapters of my life,
written in ink
that once stained my hands.

Lost Between Seconds

The long night will come,
and I am lost.
Lost in emotion,
lost in pain,
lost in time.

Time flies as the seconds
wind down the clock—
ticking—
and still, I am lost.

Lost in the clouds that fade
slowly,
as time moves on.

The long night comes
for us all.
Will it stop?
Will it stop for me?

Will it rewind the seconds
we call time?
Or am I simply lost?

So rarely does the clock reverse,
washing away
what had been said
and done.

Forward it moves—
tick and tok—until the ringing stops,
yet it goes on,
waiting…
to take the final breath
of the living.

Still we lay,
only to learn that peace
is final.

And on my last journey home,
I will turn
to rewind the clock
one final time—
for now,
I am home.

The Question That Won't Leave Me

Am I okay?

A common question
that needs to be asked—
for what, exactly,
put me on this jagged path?

Am I okay

for feeling this way?
Drinking, thinking,
tossing and turning—
these were the symptoms
of my late-night yearning.

Am I okay?

Again the question
orbits my mind
like the moon to the Earth,
constantly circling,
never drifting far behind.

Am I okay

for feeling how I feel?
My mind in two,
my heart in millions—
what could ever stop
this broken feeling?
Tears plummet
down my fractured face.

Is this a sign
that I'm okay?

Slowly, I believe
I'll never be fine—
for this is a game
played only by time.

Still,
the question rises
again and again—

Am I okay?

It's the question
that won't leave me.

The Darkness That Carried My Name

Darkness—
once a stranger in the corners of my life—
now speaks my name.
I no longer ask
if it comes as a friend
or waits as a threat.

It settled into me
as if it had always been there,
quiet, unmoving,
watching versions of myself disappear—
each one thinning into shadow,
turning to ash
before I learned
how to see what was taking me.

It taught me how to live unseen,
how to lower my voice
until silence fit like skin.
I learned my pain
by tracing it in the dark,
memorizing every place
it refused to leave.

I stopped running from what followed me
and learned to walk beside it—
not in trust,

not in fear,
but in recognition.
Because some darkness does not arrive to ruin you;
it arrives to remain,
to show you
what survives
after everything else is stripped away.

The Boy I Buried Inside Me

I buried him
where I thought no one would find him—
not because I wanted to,
but because the world taught me
softness doesn't survive long.

No one watching
as the ground settled, learning his shape,
layer after layer closing in.
I buried him for the love
I once believed was stronger
than my own mind,
convincing myself that hiding him
would make it easier
to keep moving forward
without breaking.

Who I buried was a boy
who felt too deeply,
cared too much,
cried too often,
and loved too easily.

He wasn't perfect,
and never tried to be.
He didn't know
how his softness made others
careless with him
until pain taught him
what growth demanded.

I had to bury him—
he carried hope
like it wouldn't cost him anything,
when in truth
it cost him everything he held dear.
Pain became something
you learned to live inside of.

There was a time
when a soft heart could roam freely,
but the world hardened.
And it felt safer to bury
the boy who once lived
than to stand by
and watch the world
teach him
how to disappear.

I learned to ignore his whispers,
constantly orbiting my thoughts,
wrapping my mind in vines
I once fought hard to break free from.
His weight was heavy—
but bear it I must,
and so I did.

I learned how to ration breath
while shaking inside,
how to cry without tears,
how to ache without letting it show.

Every hurt lived in my body,
yet I swallowed it whole—
afraid that feeling too deeply
might loosen the ground
I worked so hard to pack down.

So I buried the boy
that once lived.
But he refused to stay silent.

I feel him
when the nights are long—
nights damp, young, and cold.

A constant tapping from the inside,
as if he were pressing against me
with his weight,
urging me to dig up
what I left buried in the soil.

But I never answered.
Silence became the language
I learned fluently.

I built a garden
on top of his grave—
deeply rooted,
guarded,
sharp where he was gentle.

I learned to control what grew there,
gave myself the discipline
to keep it alive.
I wore thorns like armor
and called it strength—
the kind it takes
to protect everything new
I built with my hands,
no matter how many times
I mistook a wasp
for a butterfly.

In the silent moments,
when everything sits still
but the ground—
always shifting—
a song,
a memory,
a kindness given too freely
loosens the earth.

A trembling truth
the world uproots
for me to see.

I miss the boy I buried,
but I remember why
he had to stay there.
The world does not spare the weak,
and it makes no room
for soft things.

So I left the garden
and walked forward,
never needing to look back
at the grave I covered—
but always wanting to.

I survived the ever-growing weeds
by becoming someone
he never would have needed to be.And at the gates
of everything I once hoped for,
I saw only a small garden
surrounded by shadows.

I never ask
if I did the right thing—
I only ask
how much longer
a buried boy
can keep a man alive.

Still, I Stand

Here I am,
in a wave of mixed emotions.

Here I am,
standing alone in the shadows of my failures—
but here I am.

For here I am,
sliding into the world we call reality.

For here,
one gives a part of themselves to another,
only to receive betrayal in return.
But here I am.

For here,
greed and ambition outrun empathy and respect—
where love is emptied
and filled with nothing but regret.
But here I am.

Here I am,
watching compassion turn to destruction,
destruction unravel into
the annihilation of mankind.

But here,
we—mankind—watch as
mothers cry out in pain
for the ones they've lost.
And here I am.

Where boys and girls,
barely over the age of eighteen,
take their final journey home.
For there, peace is found—
gone,
yet finally within reach
of freedom.

But still,
I stand.

Ashes of the Boy I Used to Be

A candle—
a sign of celebration,
a promise of something new.
Another year added,
edging me closer
to wishing for things I could never name.

Each flame lit was a memory
marking time,
yet each candle burned
a different version of me—
one that died
the moment the smoke
touched the air.

With every blow of a candle,
I felt myself slipping away—
never the same as I was before.

The flames burned bright,
but even the shadows
smothered their light out.

Each wick held a fragment
of my younger self,
melting away before my eyes—
and still, it was celebrated.
Growing up meant losing pieces,
meant watching myself disappear,
meant eventually
stopping the candles altogether.

Time always moving against me,
carrying pieces of me
scattered across the years—
moments and faces
that no longer recognize me,
versions of myself
I only see now
in dreams.

Wishing we could've stayed that version,
often wanting to go back,
but knowing deep inside
that part of us
could no longer survive.

We had to evolve—
become someone
who could take the pain
and still blow the candles out,

pushing the ghost
made from candle smoke
onto a new journey,
far from the version
I became.

Some nights,
I still hear them in the wind,
see them in the smoke,
feel them in the shower—
the boys who couldn't remain,
wishes whispering
from the shadows
of the man I've become.

No cake,
no candles,
no gifts—
just whispers
and the fire within,
carrying the ashes
of the boy I used to be,
grateful he burned,
knowing he died
so I could survive.

SECTION III
THORNS

Pain, heartbreak, emotional weight, letting go

The Faithful and the Faithless

Filled with anger boiling inside,
tears of frustration and pain
ran down my face.
It was too much to bear—
too many lies,
too many stories,
too much to carry all at once.

Pain pounded through my fractured heart;
I knew this was only the start.
Memories roamed the open corners of my mind,
constantly replaying a terrible time.
Over and over it looped without hesitation,
reminding me of a love
that failed without salvation.

In dark rooms I lay,
watching time crawl by—
minutes into hours,
hours into days,
and I still felt the same.
Agony filled the air around me,
pushing out faith,
dragging away trust,
scraping at everything in between.

In distrust my heart beat—
damn, it hurt.
Pounding until it could take no more,
I found myself on the floor,
filled with holes
that held too much meaning.
I wish I could've stopped the bleeding—

open,
broken,
played like a fool.

Because I was the faithful—
and she was everything less.

Buried With Love

*B*eaten and bruised,
they left no clues.

I gave all I could,
and still was abused.
I hugged,
I kissed—
trying to fix
what others had missed.
Yet without remorse,
I still ended up
in that ditch.

Cold and alone,
I lay in the ground,
buried with love
but without a sound.

Giving my all
was never enough.
That pretty girl
ate my heart right up.
Craving the cuts
and bruises she gave,
I still wanted more—

for what she struck
was never the core,
and I believed

I could take a little more.
Wanting and wanting,
I begged for more,
but she did not love me
in that way anymore.

So there I fell,
alone in a hole,
sitting and singing
my tuneless song,
hoping she'd return
and play along.

And so I wait
in that lonely hole,
still singing
what I once thought
was real.

The Love That Wouldn't Leave

The feeling of love—
something I wished not to feel,
yet it came swift and silent,
unexpected and uninvited.

A love buried within me,
for the love I endured
was never what it seemed—
turning nightmares into dreams,
dreams filled with the promise
of something new,
something tender,
something almost real.

Dreams of love.
Dreams of compassion.
Oh, how I wished
that love had lasted.

It filled the air around me
with something only I could feel—
deep,
true,
and impossible to name.

Hard it was
to express the weight
that lay heavy
on my ever-changing mind.

My heart fluttered
at the thought of what could be,
yet was never mine.

And the very presence of thee
grasped my heart
only to tear it apart.

Still, the love I held
grazed my thoughts,
leaving a feeling behind
I could not let go.

in the dark it waits,
silent and patient,
making a foolish man's heart ache.

Time and time again it returns,
cursing the man
with eternal longing—

for true love is strong,
pure,
and unbreakable.

The Game I Never Win

Cold streams,
red eyes,
cries of agony—
all because of you.

Because of you,
I carry damage.
Because of you,
I bend beneath
the weight of torment,
the quiet violence
of overthinking.

I swear I won't attach—
fight the feelings,
lose anyway.
Anger screaming inward,
pain pacing my chest,
frustration with no exit.

I know you don't want me.
I like you—
I want you—
and still,
I stay committed
to a game
I never win.

Over and over
we play,
until my heart
forgets how much
it can take.

So I build a wall
to hold back the flood,
to keep the emotions
from breaking through—

and even then,
still standing,
I call myself
strong.

The First Heartbreak That Grew Me

We were young—
too young to know the weight
of the hearts we carried.
We stumbled through love
as children do,
breaking what we didn't know
how to hold.

Still, something in me
never stopped choosing you.
You were the calm in my storms,
the quiet in my chaos,
the one voice
that steadied the shaking in me.

I tried to grow fast,
to become someone worth your pride—
changing my walk,
my work,
my world—
all in the hope
that you'd see the man
I was trying to become.

I made mistakes,
left scars,
collected regret—
but my heart never wavered.
It simply learned how to beat
with the ache of wanting
what I could not hold.

Years passed,
but the truth stayed—
not the childish love we started with,
but the echo it left behind:

you were my first heartbreak,
and the reason
my heart learned
how to grow again.

The Weight I Mistook for Love

I carried the weight so long,
I forgot it wasn't love at all.
It settled into my chest
like a garden I never planted,
vines curling inward
until my heart became their soil.
Thorns threaded through every breath,
turning air into something sharp.
My hands trembled as I held on,
mistaking the sting for affection,
the pressure for closeness—
never realizing I had become
the ground it grew in,
the place where hurt learned
to make itself at home.

The longer I stood there,
the more the vines engulfed me,
mistaking me for theirs—
claiming my body as the stonewalls
they once grew upon,
overgrowing their boundaries
and enclosing me within them.
I tended to the hurt as if it were fragile,
watering it with apologies.
I chased the fertilized hope
that someone might love
what grew in this garden,
but they never took the tools
to help it grow.
And still, I believed the weight
meant devotion,
never realizing I was only feeding
what was breaking me.

There came a moment
when the weight refused to feel like love anymore.
Little by little, it changed—
hurting less in the body,
but never in the memory.
The vines that once engulfed me
tightened again,
showing me the true size of their thorns
and the sharpness I once ignored

And the breath they stole from me
returned as a warning—
a silent sign
that the garden I clung to
no longer held any life at all.
It was then I understood—
some gardens stop blooming
long before you stop trying to save them.

And so I walked away
from a garden that once held life.
I looked back only wanting
to see moments of gold,
but the truth refused
to hide itself from my eyes.
The vines unraveled from my body
the farther I went,
thorns leaving the marks
of the presence they once held—
no longer piercing,
only scraping as they lost their power.
And as the wounds began to heal,
I learned that letting go
isn't the death of love,
but the return of breath
to a body that fought to survive.

And for the first time,
I chose myself over what was killing me slowly.

THE GARDEN WHERE I BLED

In my garden were piles of roses—
roses that softened the ground beautifully,
complimenting everything they touched.
A rose is whispered as a symbol of affection,
but did we ever question
why the rose was red?

I planted these roses myself,
poured every part of me into each seed,
hoping they would bloom gently…
but someone picked with hands
that never learned to be careful.

Bloodied roses now veiled the garden—
roses touched by hands
that were never meant to be there.
Hands of greed I once mistook
for something everlasting,
now pricked by my thorns.
And in trying to save her hands,
I ruined my own—
bleeding into the soil,
watching my roses grow brighter
with every cut I took.
Every thorn cried red into the soil,
and the garden where I once loved
became the garden
where I bled.

Roses darkened from being drenched in blood,
the garden no longer echoing
with the life it once held.
Petals blackened and lifeless floated through the wind,
and the hands that once cared for this place
now carried every wound—
wounds that belonged to the garden
but were carved into me instead.

The garden became a graveyard,
filled only with memories
of what life used to be,
and in its ruins,
I found the version of myself
she'd taken without ever asking.

When the wind finally cleared the last blackened petals,
I stood in the garden I once claimed as home—
the place where I planted my roots
and grew my roses,
now overrun with weeds.
Only then did I understand
the garden was never mine to save.

the garden was never mine to save.
I had given everything I had
to a place that gave nothing back,
leaving me bleeding with the simple truth
that even the softest hearts
must learn
when to let go.

Petals Returned to the Sky

All flowers lose their petals,
one after another—
but yours were gently picked,
always taken in small pieces,
as if you'd simply grow more.

Until the soil beneath you
held more of you
than the stem
you once grew from.

The soil that once cradled
my growing seed
began to wither beneath me—
pale, stripped of richness,
its color sinking back into the earth
the way my petals once did.
Even the ground that held me
grew weak from all I gave away.

The stem once filled with color
now faded, weakened,
sinking into the earth
from which it first grew.
A flower once full of life
now feels the weight of emptiness,
as forces whip its body
one direction after another,
continuously draining
what little strength remains.

No petals left to offer,
it finally saw what it had become—
a body without a soul,
a flower stripped of everything
that once made it whole.

The fragments of its beauty,
scattered in the wind,
drifted farther than its roots
could ever reach.

All that remained
was the core from which it grew,
a flower bowing low,
remembering its days
in the sun.

A life
once full,
now torn from you—
its pieces taken,
a sign you gave
everything you had.

What little you held
returned to the dirt,
as all things will—
a seed to the earth,
as your petals
to the sky,
a quiet reminder
that pieces of ourselves
will always rise.

The Day She Comes Home

When she's ready,
she'll find me in the place she left me—
waiting, but no longer the man she left,
hardened like cement,
forgotten and covered in vines.

When she's ready…
If she ever found her way back,
I'd hold her heart and feel her beat—
I'd carry no mistakes against her,
not even the ones born
from our damaged past,
worn out from the grief
her absence carved into me.

Like water to rock,
she wore me down—
digging deep
and corroding
what remained of me.

Worn and misshaped,
chiseled by someone I once knew,
I reformed
and became someone new.

Time reshaped me,
so I understand her now.
My love was buried deep
in the version we outgrew—
yet still, my heart reaches
for the love it once knew.
But when she's ready,
I'll be waiting too—
not for who she was,
but for who she'd become too.

And when she's ready,
she'll find her way home—
changed,
not broken,
healed from her absence,
yet still longing
for my presence.

When I Finally Let Go

When I finally let go,
it wasn't the garden that saved me—
not the soil,
not even my roots.
The thorns had always been there,
small enough to ignore,
but sharp enough to carve into me.
They grew through every wound
until the bleeding became a quiet routine.
I let go because I grew tired
of pretending I couldn't feel myself break.

It took time to see the truth:
not every garden grows you—
some only teach you how to bleed.
I grew used to the stabbing sensation,
the burn of every cut,
the kind of hurt you pretend is nothing
until it becomes everything.
And in this garden,
there was nothing left for me—
nothing but the scars etched into my hands
and a single rose gripped too tightly.
Fist closed,
blood running from my palm,
I finally accepted the pain
and let the rose fall.
And letting it go
hurt less than holding on ever did.

As the rose fell to the ground,
silence rose around me—
an unfamiliar truth no one warns you about.
Letting go did hurt less,
yet the memories carved their wound deep into my body,
refusing to fade.
But releasing the rose
made space for someone new to grow—
someone no longer trapped
in a garden that fed on their pain.
I didn't know who I was
without something to cling to,
but the absence of hurt
felt, for the first time,
like the beginning of breathing again.

Every step I took away from the garden
signaled a new beginning—
a new strength,
a different kind of feeling.
The soil remained firm,
the roses still dead,
but my body no longer watered those places.
The hands that once cared for the garden were gone,
yet the heart I poured into it
remained bloodied—
but no longer begging to be saved.

Leaving the garden taught me
that survival was never found in holding on—
it lived in the courage to leave.
And with every step further,
I thought of every petal I lost
and every piece of myself I gained.
In that quiet distance,
I felt myself slowly returning
to the person I was meant to become.

Because sometimes the only way to save yourself
is to stop bleeding for what won't grow.

SECTION IV
BLOOM

Growth with scars

What Am I?

What am I?
Only a few will truly know.
I wait in the dark,
yet somehow, I'm never alone.

Soft at times,
but hard when I have to be.
Sometimes quiet,
other times loud—
still you look at me
and struggle to see.

Blue flowing in,
red rushing out…
without me, you're gone—
of that, there's no doubt.

Countless connections,
I rely on them all.
Supporting the body is my duty—
steady at rest,
racing when you fall.

What am I?
Still unsure?
Full or empty
in a single beat—
how strange that sounds,
how strangely true.

how strangely true.
The center of a system,
I can't go missing.Lose me,
and life disappears in a flash,
or slows to a siren's cry
within minutes.

Warm as a hug,
cold as a shoulder.
As beautiful as a flower,
but as essential as roots.

So tell me—
what am I, really?
What are these pieces,
these pulses and truths,
that make me…
me?

Rips and Tears

Every rip,
every tear,
teaches my body to grow
in places my mind
was too slow to understand.

I am a beast—
and these muscles will grow,
watered by nothing
but my own determination.
The results will show soon—
proof of my will,
my hunger,
and my power.

It's never been about praise
or the stories they'll make.
I fight myself every day
just to see if I'm better
than I was yesterday—
even if the progress
was only an inch.

The process is slow,
never meant
for full display.
Pain is the price I pay
to build a better version
of myself someday—
past the breaking points,
beneath whatever glory
they think they see.

The proof is in the work,
not the words.

Push yourself—
the beast lives within.

Trained and Disciplined

I used to follow the footsteps
of those who marched long before me—
long days, short nights,
and early mornings built into my bones.
This was the structure laid before me,
and I improved it with purpose.

Strongly built and well-defended,
I fortified myself along the way.
I learned that discipline doesn't happen overnight,
nor from orders followed without doubt—
but from the courage that is forged,
the courage it takes
to confront one's own mistakes
and that of others.

This is discipline,
and I was forged for it.
Built for it—
a seed blossomed into a tree,
deeply rooted yet ever growing,
always rising, always changing.
This is my life.

Now I fall into formation,
not as a soldier, but as a leader—
trained and proficient in my warrior skills,
a product of time, sweat,
and self-discipline.
A fight not only within,
but for the nation.

Stitched Into Me

I wear my name
not because I choose it,
but because it's what I have.

Dragged through the dirt
in which we call time,
aged but no better
than fine wine.
I played my role,
but that part of me
had to die —
a vision built in silence
and alone time.

This struggle we carry isn't ours alone,
many in a family so far from home,
many in search of a place to belong —
but this one is personal, so there'll be no songs,
battles fought in silence
where the blood never shows,
where nights are heavy
and pain travels alone.

Through the pain and struggle, you stayed,
and I think I've found the one
to carry my name.

Through every rain, through every storm,
in which we sheltered in one another.
So I place my name in your hands,
not for you to hold,
but for us to carry —
together,
unbroken.

The Beauty That Healed Me

Beautiful in her soul—
that's the way I loved her.
Beautiful as a whole—
there was no other.

Beautiful like Mother Nature,
she did it naturally,
filling me with euphoria
so effortlessly.

Sweet on a tongue
that once tasted bitter,
she grew like the flowers
that survived the winter.

Peace she brought me
every time she was near.
Deep were the thoughts
I dwelled on—
some even brought me tears.

A piece of her mind
was all I ever craved.
Beautiful in her thoughts,
she could drive you insane.
In my mind,
she was always the same—
beautiful and confident,
and I liked her that way.

Elegant she was;
she always did it best.
Her scent filled the room
as I began to decompress.

She was beautiful
in a way that never
compared to the rest.
Beautiful to me—
that's how I loved her best.

So beautiful to me…
my eyes near rest.

Rich in All the Ways That Matter

I want a rich girl—
not silver nor gold,
but one who still shines
when the world grows cold.

I want a rich girl—
beautiful and strong,
the kind who lifts me
when everything feels wrong.

I want a rich girl
with heart and soul,
someone to hold
when the nights grow long.

I want a rich girl—
sweet, yet full of fire,
a steady flame
when my own burns tired.

I want a rich girl
who dreams out loud,
who's selfish at times,
yet grounded and proud.

I want a rich girl
who wants me, not needs me,
who learned her worth
before standing beside me.

I want a rich girl—
rich in love and fight,
the kind of love
that makes life feel right.

I want a rich girl—
not diamond nor stone,
but one who feels like home,
where a man can grow old.

Love Me

Love me—
I used to give it out so easily,
never realizing what it was worth.
Always forgetting to love myself,
always searching for the next one
while trying to find home.

Love me—
I begged those who were only searching
for keys to their own song,
forgetting my heart came from a broken home,
forgetting I was still learning
right from wrong.

Love me—
I never spoke the words,
but you could hear them
in every song I sang.
I forgot that was just the way I was,
but I never forgot
that was the way I felt—
"Love me"
a quiet cry for help.

But after long silence,
I found myself,
loving the parts
no one stayed long enough
to see.

Love me—
I whispered to myself,
realizing I never needed anyone else,
just the rhythm and the beat
of my one true self.

Love me—
was no longer a plea,
just a memory
of who I was
and how I felt.

I love me now.
Love yourself
before trying
to love someone else.

Fearing Shadows

I fear the shadows
for what they may hold—
long in wait,
quiet and cold.
The shadows do not fear me;
they've studied my weakness
from the shadows within,
breaking me with silence.
Now I can admit.

I lived in the shadows
I grew used to,
feeling like a friend
I went to school with.
They knew me well—
one foot bigger than the other—
they brought me comfort
and made me feel content.

The light—
a sun blazing danger,
burning away the fear
I had grown used to.
I dared not step into it.
I wasn't ready,
but the world was ready
to see me healed,
opened to opportunity,
and ready to watch me
bask in its light.

I trembled before the light,
uncertain of the manit would reveal,
but I refused to let it win.
So I stepped forward anyway,
letting its warmth
settle into my skin,
soaking in its rays
like someone learning
they were meant to shine too.

And for the first time,
the light didn't scare me—
it welcomed me.

The Boy Who Learned to Grow

I remember the boy I was
by the posture of his silence—
by the ashes
he buried in the ground.

He carried weight in quiet,
enough to pass for strength.

He stayed when seasons hardened,
stood inside unnamed cold—
trembling, still upright.

He moved forward
without asking the ground.

Growth came slowly.
Not as arrival—
as return.

The same days,
the same work,
hands learning
the cost of staying.

Roots took
without announcement.
Change happened
where no one looked.

He stopped measuring himself
by what was lost.
By what remained—
the courage to grow,
the resolve to stay rooted,
the strength to endure.

It was enough.
Still becoming.

The first sprout.

ABOUT THE AUTHOR

Omarion G. Phillips
was born on April 29, 2003,
in Jacksonville, Florida, and
raised in the heart of Orlando.
At twenty-two years old,
he writes with a voice shaped
by struggle, silence, and the
kind of growth that comes from surviving what was
never spoken aloud.

The middle ground of a family with multiple siblings,
Omarion learned early what it meant to carry weight quietly.
His work is built from the soil of his own becoming—the pain
he transformed, the battles he outgrew, and the resilience
he learned to shape with his hands.

His poetry is known for its depth, its honesty, and its
unflinching voice. Through grounded imagery and emotional
truth, he writes for those who have been buried by life but still
found a way to rise. His words carry the heartbeat of someone
who has broken, rebuilt, and bloomed — again and again.

What grew was never meant to stop.

ACKNOWLEDGMENTS

To every moment and every person who waited for me
blossom, even when I couldn't see the growth in myself.
even who for holding on when I broke in silence,
—thank you for holding on when I broke in silence,
when my self-worth felt fragile,
when I almost pulled myself from the ground entirely.

To the people who saw something in me, before I ever
saw it in myself, who reminded me that even the
wounded bloom when given time, light, and patience.

To the memories that hardened me, the one who survived
what he never spoke about—this book is proof
that you made it.

Thanks,
Omarion Phillips